I0797962

BOSS

THE GLAND FACTORY

RACHEL POLIQUIN
ILLUSTRATIONS BY
CLAYTON HANMER

THE GLAND FACTORY

A TOUR OF YOUR BODY'S GOOPS, JUICES, AND HORMONES

GREYSTONE KIDS
GREYSTONE BOOKS • VANCOUVER/BERKELEY/LONDON

CONTENTS

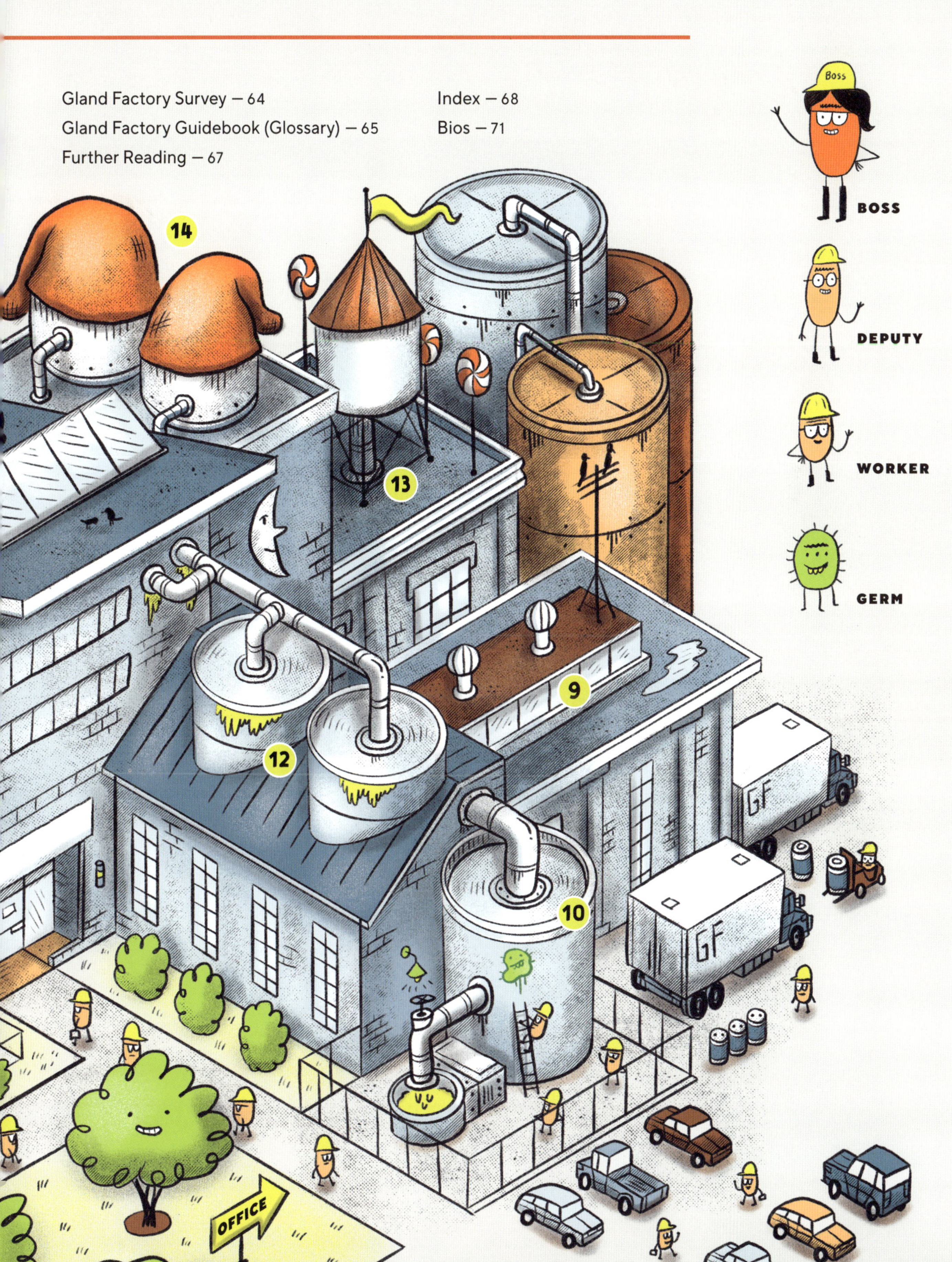
Boss
BOSS
DEPUTY
WORKER
GERM
14
13
12
9
10
GF
GF
OFFICE

I know what you're thinking. You're thinking, *What the heck is a Gland Factory, and why do I have one?*

These are good questions. Smart questions. So get ready for some keen and clever answers. Because what you are about to see will guarantee you never think about snot or pee or doughnuts the same way again.

What you are about the learn is so amazing, it will blow the hair right off your chest. And before you say you don't have any chest hair, you should know, whether you do or don't, it's all controlled right here in the Gland Factory. We control *everything*—whether you cry or grow or feel hungry or build bones or sweat or pee or sleep or feel so nervous you just might puke. It's all us. Doing all of that.

But *how*? I'm sure that's your next question. How can your **glands** be so important when you barely knew they existed?

Let me explain it like this: Imagine a duck swimming across a pond. It seems to glide so peacefully through the water—no sweat, no effort. But have you ever seen what's going on *under* the water to keep that duck gliding so smoothly? The ceaseless paddling? The frenzied flippering? The never-ending tiny readjustments to stay on course?

My friends, you are a lot like that duck.

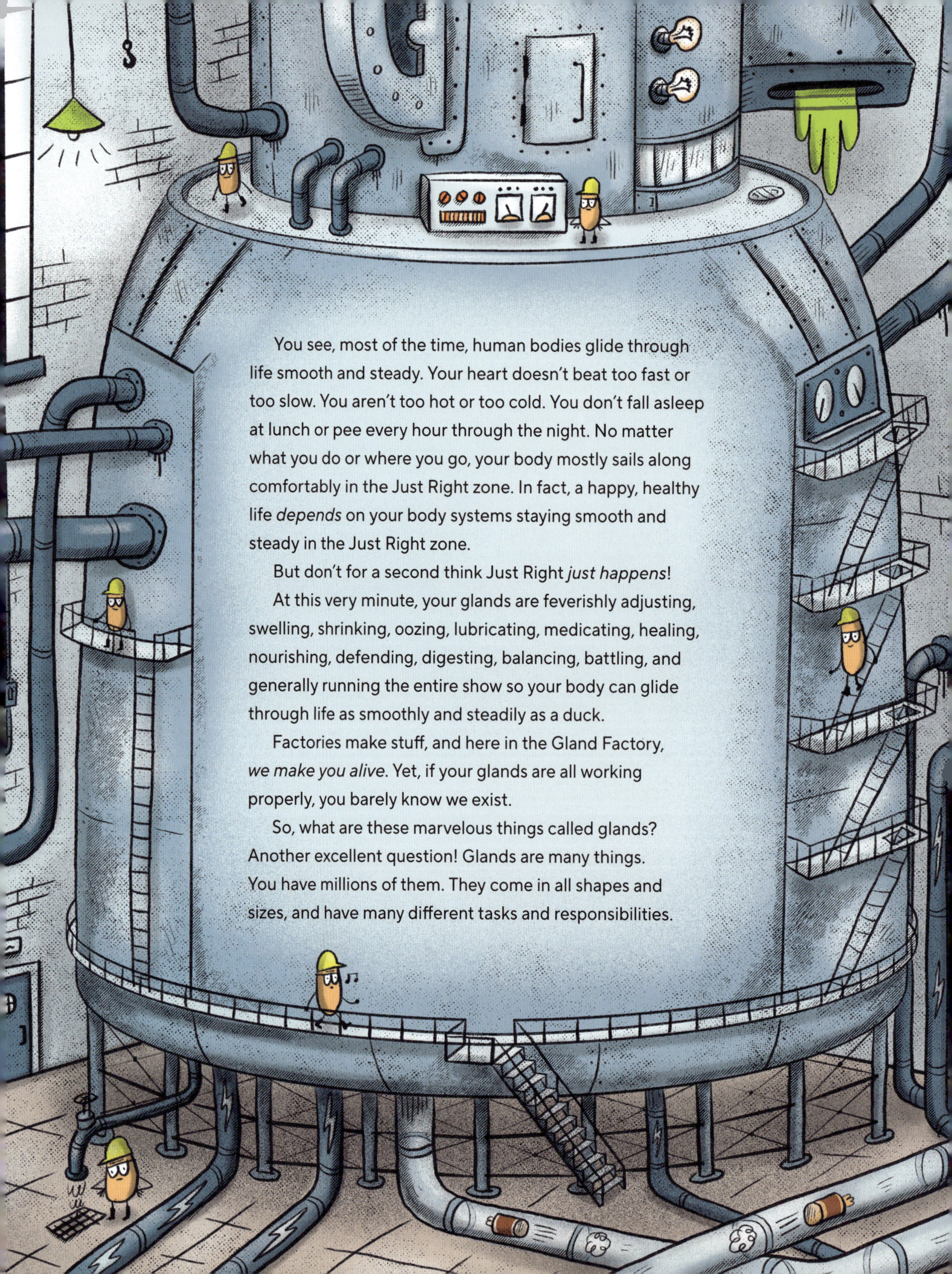

You see, most of the time, human bodies glide through life smooth and steady. Your heart doesn't beat too fast or too slow. You aren't too hot or too cold. You don't fall asleep at lunch or pee every hour through the night. No matter what you do or where you go, your body mostly sails along comfortably in the Just Right zone. In fact, a happy, healthy life *depends* on your body systems staying smooth and steady in the Just Right zone.

But don't for a second think Just Right *just happens*!

At this very minute, your glands are feverishly adjusting, swelling, shrinking, oozing, lubricating, medicating, healing, nourishing, defending, digesting, balancing, battling, and generally running the entire show so your body can glide through life as smoothly and steadily as a duck.

Factories make stuff, and here in the Gland Factory, *we make you alive*. Yet, if your glands are all working properly, you barely know we exist.

So, what are these marvelous things called glands? Another excellent question! Glands are many things. You have millions of them. They come in all shapes and sizes, and have many different tasks and responsibilities.

SOME GLANDS ARE SO SMALL THEY ARE ALMOST INVISIBLE.
LIKE SWEAT GLANDS.
SOME GLANDS ARE LARGE AND LUMPY.
LIKE THE LIVER.
SOME GLANDS MAKE GOOP LIKE SNOT, TEARS, OR MILK. WE CALL THESE THE GOOP GLANDS.
OFFICIALLY, THEY'RE EXOCRINE GLANDS.
SOME GLANDS SEND MESSAGES AROUND YOUR BODY. THESE ARE THE MESSENGER GLANDS.
OFFICIALLY, THEY'RE ENDOCRINE GLANDS. THEY SEND SPECIAL MESSAGES CALLED HORMONES TO KEEP YOUR BODY SYSTEMS WORKING TOGETHER IN HARMONY.
AND SOME GLANDS MAKE BOTH GOOP AND MESSAGES. WE CALL THESE GLANDS AMAZING!
I CAN'T ARGUE WITH THAT!
CAUTION HOT!
BOSS

As you can imagine, the Gland Factory is *huge*. Just look at all these departments! We can only see the highlights today—touring the entire factory would take weeks, and I'm far too busy for that. Here is a guidebook with extra details and a map, in case you get lost. But please don't get lost. We will be moving quickly.

Lastly, all visitors must wear safety suits and goggles to support our **NO GO IN** security system. That means **NO G**erms or **O**ther **I**nvading **N**asties allowed—especially the 3 Ds: disease, dirt, and dryness. Of course, nasties do sometimes sneak in and cause the queasies, coughs, and chills. But your Infection Detection Immune System will make sure they don't stay long.

Now, step inside the impossibly complex, life-sustaining wonderland that is your Gland Factory!

Our tour begins with the world-famous Mouth Machine! But blisters and bunions! It's already working. We can't get in—those teeth could crunch you dead. But we're here, so let's talk saliva.

I'm sure you know how the Mouth Machine works with its tearing, munching, and crunching. And, of course, the swallowing. All very impressive. But who do you think keeps the machine in tiptop shape? The Gland Factory, of course! Specifically, your salivary glands.

Your **salivary glands** make saliva, also known as spit. No surprise there. But what you may not know is that without saliva your Mouth Machine would go kaput—it would be a dried-up, broken-down hunk of junk. Actually, it would be worse than that. Without saliva, your mouth would be a House of Horrors: brown teeth, rotten gums, mouth sores, shriveled taste buds, cracked lips, endless pain, choking, even bad breath.

You see, saliva is one of your body's Defender Goops. Defender Goops are the front line of your NO GO IN security system and cover all parts of your body where Insides meet Outside.

Defender Goops are made by the Goop Glands. Not all Goop Glands make Defender Goop—some make milk, bile, or sweat—but the glands that do protect your insides from invading nasties all day every day.

Lucky for you, your mouth is filled with salivary glands. Most are too tiny to see. A few are larger and lumpy. The biggest duo, the parotid glands, are about the size of baby potatoes. They're located just in front of your ears.

THE GLAND FACTORY

THE GOOP GLANDS

Goop Glands, also known as the **exocrine glands**, make special kinds of liquids like saliva, tears, mucus, milk, sweat, and digestive juices.

All Goop Glands have a sac to make their goop and a tube, or duct, to carry the goop where it needs to go.

But big or little, salivary glands make saliva, even at night, and especially when you eat—more than 4 cups (1 liter) every day!—so your entire mouth is eternally soaked in a protective goopy shield.

Not only does saliva fight germs while keeping your mouth pleasantly moist, but it's also filled with painkillers, cleans your teeth, and prevents acids from burning holes in them. It helps grind food into mush, begins digesting that mush, and stops the mush from getting stuck as it goes down your esophagus. And let's not forget your taste buds—saliva helps keep them moist and healthy, and dissolves food so your taste buds can experience all the flavors. No saliva, no taste. Just a mouth full of misery and bad bacteria.

KNOW YOUR SIGNS + SYSTEMS
SALIVA LEVELS
JUST RIGHT
DROOLING
Food is coming. Mouth is preparing.
DRY
Body low on water. Drink!
SALIVA TSUNAMI
Warning! Puke alert! Vomit is very acidic and can burn teeth and gums. Mouth is protected by extra saliva.
TOO DRY TO SWALLOW
Peril! Fear! Saliva is cut off to focus on immediate dangers.
The GLAND FACTORY
WE'LL BE TALKING MORE ABOUT THIS LATER.
BOSS

Welcome to your nostril! If you've ever stuck your finger inside (and I know you have), you already know the most important nostril fact: it's wet in here. Sometimes it flows like a river. Sometimes it's stuck with gummy bits. But the inside of a nostril is always at least a little damp.

Dampness may not seem like much of much. But never underestimate a damp nostril!

The nostril is the body's main entrance for air, unless you're a mouth breather. And as you probably know, the coming in and going out of air is important.

And yet, air is dirty. Most of the time, you can't see the dirt, but air is thick with dust, germs, bacteria, pollen, and all sorts of nasties. It's also dry—and your lungs don't like dry air at all. So, what's a nostril to do? Wash the air with snot! You're coming in, so you'll need a wash too.

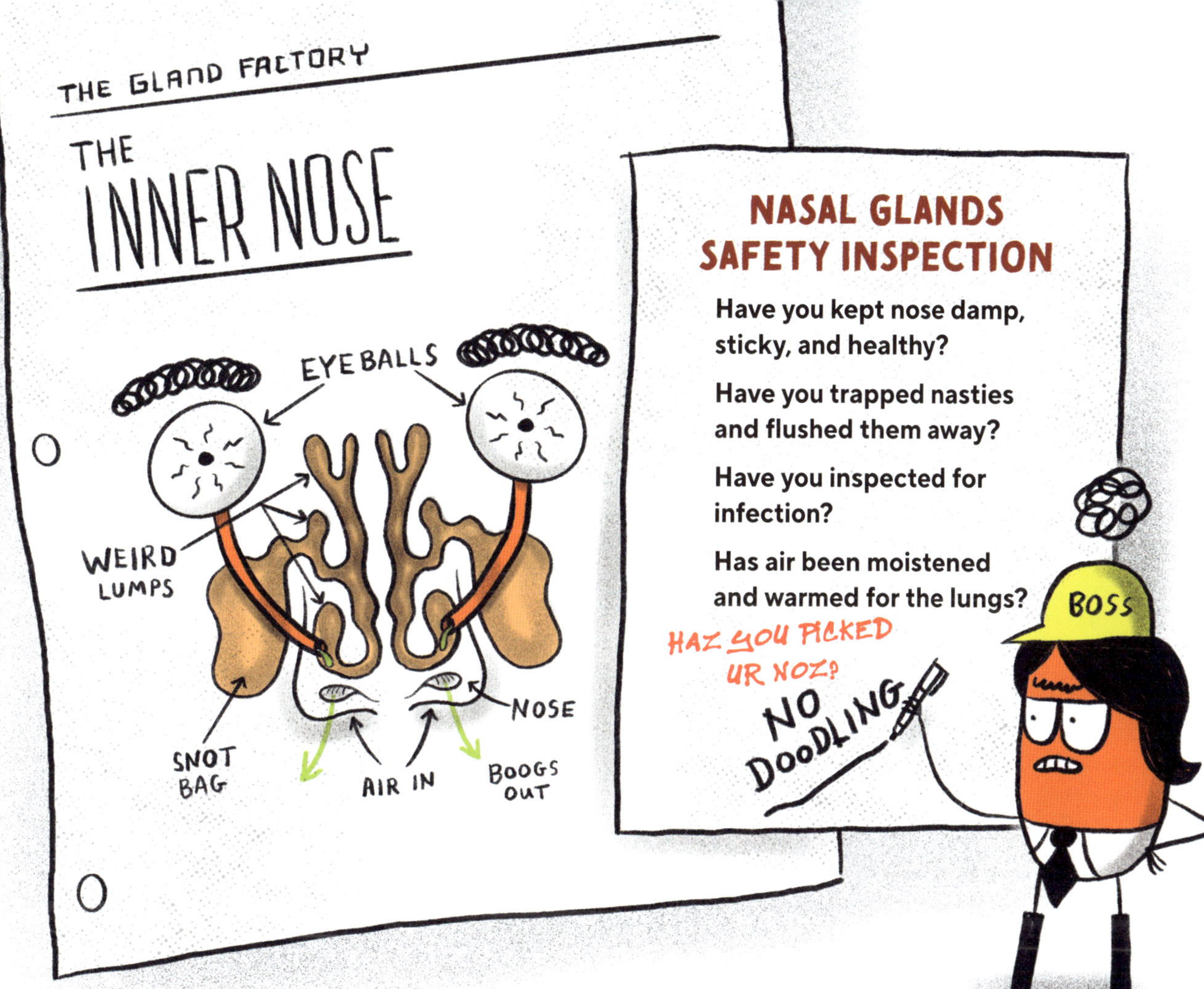

As you can see, each nostril is outfitted with nozzles and hairs. These nozzles are your **nasal glands**, and they have one and only one job: to ooze snot. Another Defender Goop! All day every day, your nasal nozzles ooze a continuous dribble of snot—properly called **mucus**—so that the entire inside of your nose, including each and every hair, remains forever sticky and damp.

Your inner nose is far bigger than what you can feel with your finger. Inside is a maze-like cavern filled with strange lumps and squeezy passages, all covered in nasal nozzles and hairs. You actually have two kinds of nose hairs: the big ones you can see and itsy-bitsy-almost-invisible ones called cilia. Together, the big hairs, the itsy-bitsy cilia, the nasal nozzles, and your weird inner-nose architecture all work together to create the most impressive, scientifically superior defense system against nasty intruders the world has ever seen. We call it the Snot Shower!

Here's how it works. As you breathe in, air is forced to spin around the lumps and through the squeezy passages, which slows the air down so it can be warmed and moistened for the lungs. All the squeezing and spinning also lets the Snot Shower work its magic. The big hairs catch the big stuff like dust and pollen—you sneeze most of this out. The itsy-bitsy cilia catch tiny things such as germs.

The whole system is like a carwash, but with snot-sticky hairs instead of soapy brushes. The hairs wrap the nasties in mucus and pass them backward to your throat. Then you swallow them. It's gross, but once the nasties hit your stomach acid (the same acid that could burn holes in your teeth, if it weren't for your saliva), they're knocked dead on contact. Mucus also—

Phew! That was a close one. Where was I? Oh yes ... mucus. It really is a wonder. It protects the entire inside of your respiratory system, from your nostrils all the way down into your lungs. If your nose or lungs ever do get infected, we crank open the snot nozzles to swamp the germs and flush them out.

Mucus! The Ultimate Defender Goop! I could talk about it all day. I won't. The tour must go on. There is so much to see. Speaking of which, on to the eyeballs!

MUCUS COLOR CODE

KNOW YOUR SIGNS + SYSTEMS

CODE CLEAR	CODE WHITE	CODE YELLOW	CODE GREEN	CODE RED	CODE BROWN	CODE BLACK
All fine	**Possible infection**	**Battling an infection** The color comes from dead fighter cells	**Worsening infection** Even more dead fighter cells	**Nosebleed** Dry nose Hydrate with cream	**Dried blood or dirt** Yicky	**Possible fungal infection** See doctor

THE JELLY BALLS

THE LACRIMAL GLANDS

Your eyeballs have lots of glands, and they all have fancy names. The least fancy in the group are the **lacrimal glands**, which is still a pretty fancy way of saying "The Glands That Do the Weeping." But the others have names like the Glands of Zeis, the Glands of Wolfring, and the Crypts of Henle. Fantastic! There's the Glands of Manz and the Glands of Moll. Who comes up with this stuff?

But the point is not their fancy names. The point is: why so many different eyeball glands?

It's because they all make *different sorts* of Defender Goops. And, even more fabulous, the different goops don't blend together; they stay in *separate layers*, one on top of the other, to literally coat your eyeballs in layers of protection. Wow.

YOUR EYEBALL GLANDS WERE MOSTLY NAMED AFTER OLD EYEBALL SCIENTISTS.

You see, your eyeballs aren't protected with the waterproof, germ-proof skin that covers most of your body—if they were, you wouldn't be able to see. Instead, you have two wet jelly balls that are constantly open to the Outside (except except while blinking and snoozing), and so are constantly being battered with dust, germs, pollen, twigs, wind, itchy things, and the never-ending deathly dryness of air. Your eyeballs defend against all of that all day long while still capturing the world like your own personal movie. Double wow.

So, what's in these marvelous layers?

The first layer, closest to the eyeball, is mucin, the main ingredient of mucus. Mucin is good at sticking things together—it holds the layers of wetness onto your eyeballs and also stops nasties from attaching. The next layer is made of tears: they're watery and salty and filled with nutrients and germ fighters to keep your eyeballs clean, wet, and healthy. Finally, the outermost layer is made up of two oily liquids called sebum and—

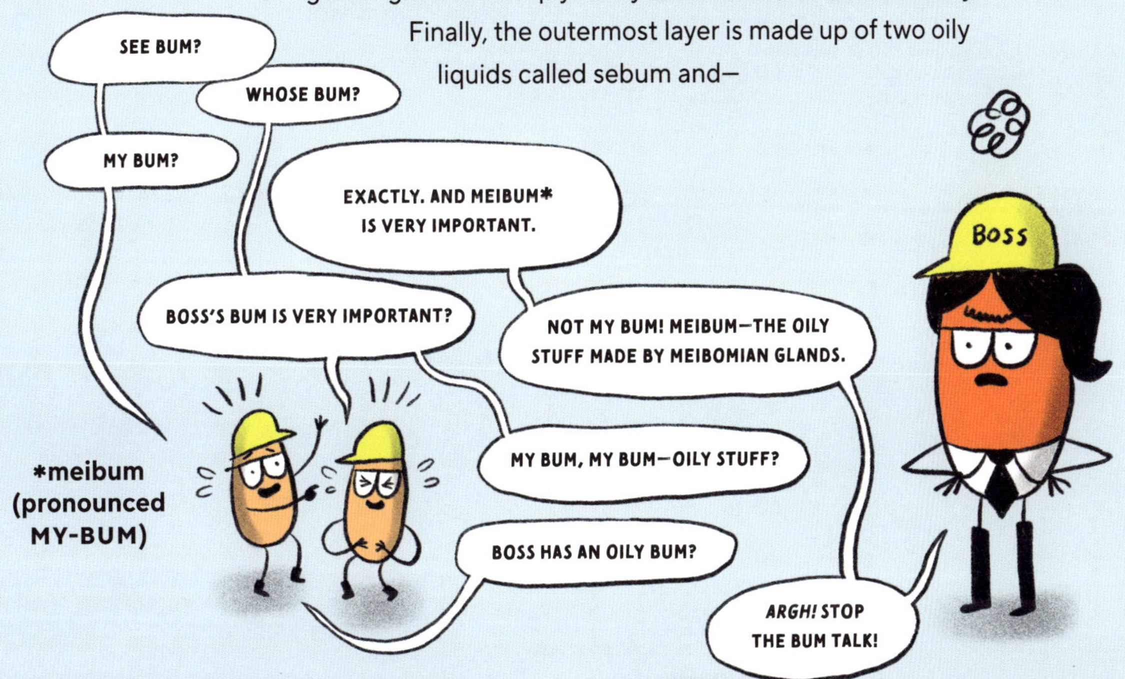

***meibum (pronounced MY-BUM)**

The outermost oily layer (made of meibum and sebum) is crucial. Every time you blink, your glands squeeze out a little oil; every time you open your eyes again, the oil spreads across the watery tears to keep them from evaporating.

So far, this tour has explored the edges of your body and the Defender Goop that keeps dirt, germs, and dryness out. But your Gland Factory is about much more than goop. So much more!

Just step through these doors and see for yourself. Please stay close and don't touch *anything*.

GERMZ
RULE

Welcome to your Insides! All of this is going on inside you at each and every moment of your life. Amazing, isn't it?

Follow me to Main Control. That's where we'll get a better understanding of what's going on.

MAIN CONTROL

THE HYPOTHALAMUS

Here we are, in the center of it all—the **hypothalamus**, Main Control, the headquarters, the hub.

From here, we monitor and regulate the basic bodily functions that keep you alive, like your breathing, heart rate, water and salt levels, hunger, temperature, growth, and puberty. The hypothalamus also initiates Panic Mode and Sleep Mode. And it makes sure all your systems keep working together as an incredible interconnected factory of life. In short, the hypothalamus is very, very impressive.

But still, you may be thinking, *Where's the goop?*

Well, there isn't any. Not here. The hypothalamus isn't a Goop Gland. It's a *Messenger* Gland.

You see, the Gland Factory has two separate divisions. There are the Goop Glands that make snot, saliva, sweat, and such. And there are the Messenger Glands. The Messenger Glands, as their name suggests, send and receive a continuous stream of messages around your body with the sole purpose of keeping you alive.

How exactly do messages keep you alive?

Well, take a look at the hypothalamus's main control panels. To live a happy, healthy life, these dials must remain within the Just Right zone. Scientists call this homeostasis, which means *keeping all body systems stable and running steady no matter what changes or utter pandemonium may be happening all around.* (That's the official definition. You can look it up.)

To keep your body stable, your hypothalamus needs to know everything that is happening everywhere at all times. Is your skin getting hot? Is it getting dark outside? How quickly are you digesting that doughnut? How much salt or sugar is in your blood? Is there something scary out there? Is your heart beating too fast? Too slow? Are your ankles swelling? What color is your pee? Have you grown enough this month? So much information!

Your hypothalamus is just a pea-sized gland deep inside your brain, so how can it possibly know all these things?

Messages! All day every day, your hypothalamus gets a constant stream of updates from your body parts. If it detects even the tiniest shift away from Just Right, it fires off its own messages to get you back on track.

I cannot stress this enough: *these dials must be kept steady!* Homeostasis means life, and keeping you alive is the Gland Factory's one and only job. Even a small shift in one system—like your water levels—can start a cascade of trouble across all systems.

If it sounds incredibly complicated, that's because it is!

To get a better idea of how it all works, let's have a look at one of the simpler systems: your Temperature Control.

THE MESSENGER GLANDS

The Messenger Glands, also known as **~~endocrine~~ glands**, are part of a ~~wondrous~~ network of glands, organs, and tissues that supervise, stabilize, and coordinate the body's vital systems, including digestion, blood circulation, growth, sleep, energy, temperature, metabolism, reproduction, and the body's response to injury, stress, disease, and germs.

TEMPERATURE CONTROL
R
L
THERMOREGULATION
98.6°F
98.2°F
97.4°F
INSTA ZAP

Behold—the main panel for Temperature Control! It's connected to temperature sensors all over your body, and it also monitors the temperature of your blood. As you can see, your body likes to be around 98.6°F (37°C). Once your temperature goes up or down, even a little, something needs to happen to get you back to Just Right. We call it thermoregulation.

If your temperature drops, Main Control initiates Warm-Up Mode. It sends messages to start your muscles shivering (which makes heat) and to shrink blood vessels in your outer ranges—such as your hands and feet and even your skin's surface (which slows heat loss by keeping more hot blood in the center of your body).

But today is hot. Our sensors tell us you're hot. We have already initiated Cool-Down Mode. We've ordered your **sweat glands**—more Goop Glands, and about 3 million of them!—to begin oozing to cool your skin.

So how do we send all these orders? Messages! So many messages! To send and receive messages, your body needs a message delivery system. It doesn't have one.

It has two!

> **KNOW YOUR SIGNS + SYSTEMS**
>
> ## TEMPERATURE CONTROL
>
> **HOT RESPONSE:**
> Sweat, swollen hands and feet, red face
>
> **Speed up heat loss:**
> Blood vessels expand near body's surface to carry more blood to the skin to offload more heat.
>
> **Lose heat:**
> As sweat evaporates off skin, it takes heat with it.
>
> **COLD RESPONSE:**
> Blue lips, chattering teeth, shivering
>
> **Slow down heat loss:** Blood vessels near surface constrict to keep more hot blood in the center. Keeping heart, lungs, and brain at the right temperature is more important that warm toes.
>
> **Make heat:** Muscles rapidly squeeze and relax (shivering).

YOUR NERVOUS SYSTEM AND YOUR BLOOD!

Your Gland Factory uses two very different message delivery systems. The first is your nervous system—a whole-body, lightning-fast communication network that functions like electrical cables connecting every bit of your body to your brain.

The second is your blood. Your heart pumps blood around your body through your blood vessels, delivering good stuff and removing bad stuff to and from each and every cell.

These two systems may seem the same-ish, but they are not the same. Not at all.

Your nervous system only delivers messages. It delivers them directly, and at electric speed—Insta-Zap! We already saw this at work with your Temperature Control. Your hypothalamus sent electrical messages to your blood vessels to expand and to your sweat glands to sweat. Direct and instant.

Your blood doesn't work like this at all. It's more like a pool party in a looping stream. It isn't direct, it isn't fast, and it carries so much more than messages. All sorts of things are bobbling along in your blood: red and white blood cells, nutrients, gases, salt, proteins ... so much stuff.

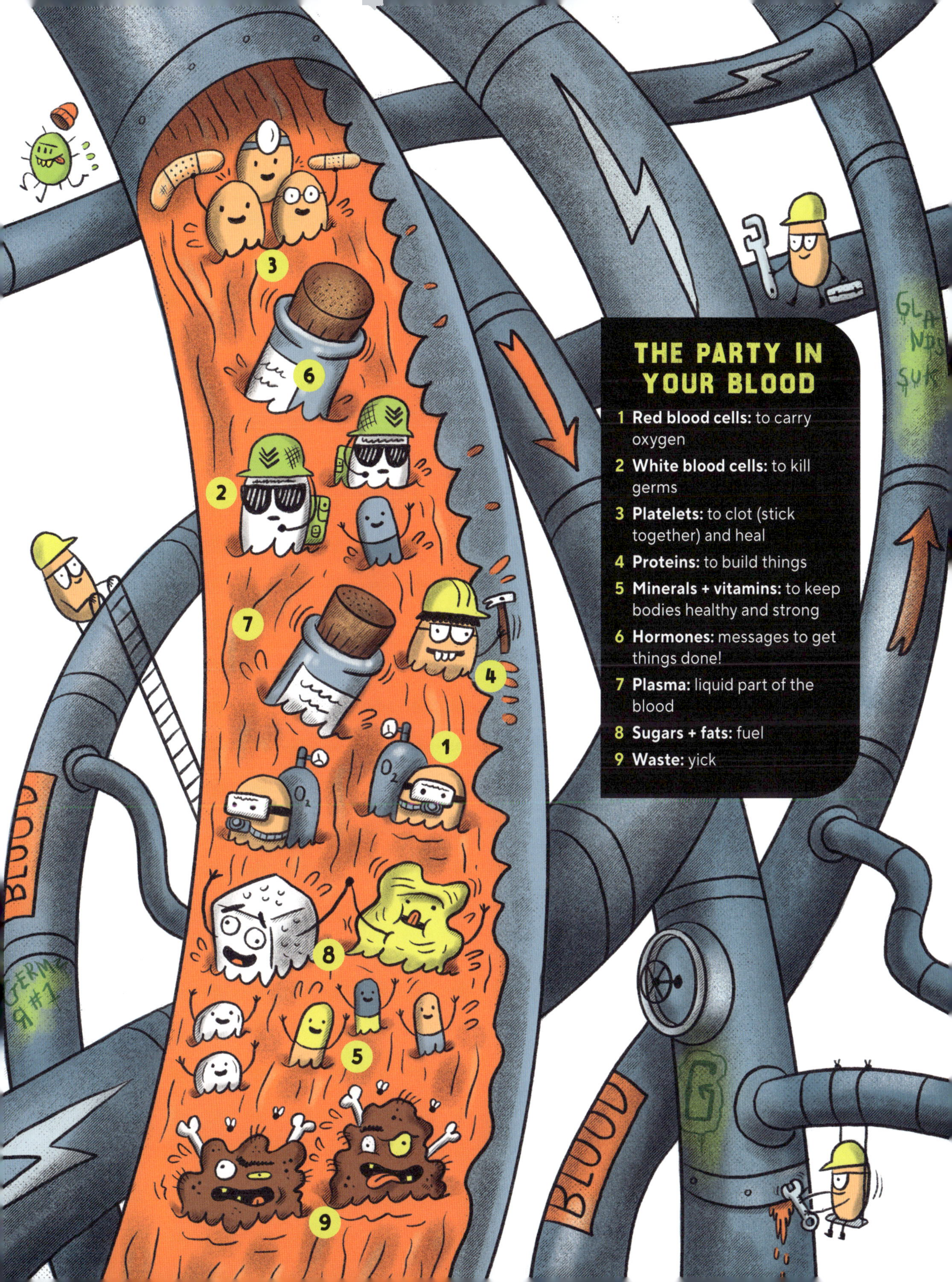
THE PARTY IN YOUR BLOOD
1 Red blood cells: to carry oxygen
2 White blood cells: to kill germs
3 Platelets: to clot (stick together) and heal
4 Proteins: to build things
5 Minerals + vitamins: to keep bodies healthy and strong
6 Hormones: messages to get things done!
7 Plasma: liquid part of the blood
8 Sugars + fats: fuel
9 Waste: yick
BLOOD
BLOOD

Here's how your blood messages work. When a Messenger Gland needs to communicate with other body parts, it pops its message into your bloodstream.

Then it waits.

Your blood burbles along with all its bits and bobs, and eventually the message passes the right body part. That body part reads the message and does whatever it's been commanded to do. Not direct. Not instant. But much more widespread and longer-lasting than the Insta-Zap messages delivered by your nerves. I'll explain more about this in a moment.

But first, a few words about these blood-traveling messages. They have a special name: hormones. Many people know hormones as the chemicals that give teenagers pimples and help mothers grow babies. But hormones are so much more than that!

Hormones control your heartbeat, how sleepy you feel, and whether your arms are the same length. They control how thirsty or hairy you are, how peppy or pukey you feel, how tall, hungry, constipated, salty, muscly, or bone-breakable you are. Hormones do all of it! And yet, most people think all hormones are sex hormones. I just don't understand it.

Now, here is a question: If all these messages are bubbling along, passing each of the 30 trillion cells in your body—Whoa. That's a lot of cells!—how does the right message get delivered to the right cell?

It's wonderfully clever. I can't wait to explain. Let's head down these stairs, and I'll show you how it works.

TRAPPED BY HORMONE STEREOTYPES?
YOU ARE SO MUCH MORE THAN PIMPLES & BABIES
H
YOU DO ALL THE THINGS!
DROWSY • HUNGRY • HAPPY • THIRSTY • SWEATY • SNOOZY
PANICKY • HAIRY • BIG-BONED • LONG-LEGGED •
POOPY • SALTY • GRUMPY • HEARTBURNY
TIRED • ANGRY • EXCITED
BOSS
HYPOTHALAMUS
UP HERE
IN YO FACE GLAND CHUMPZ!!!

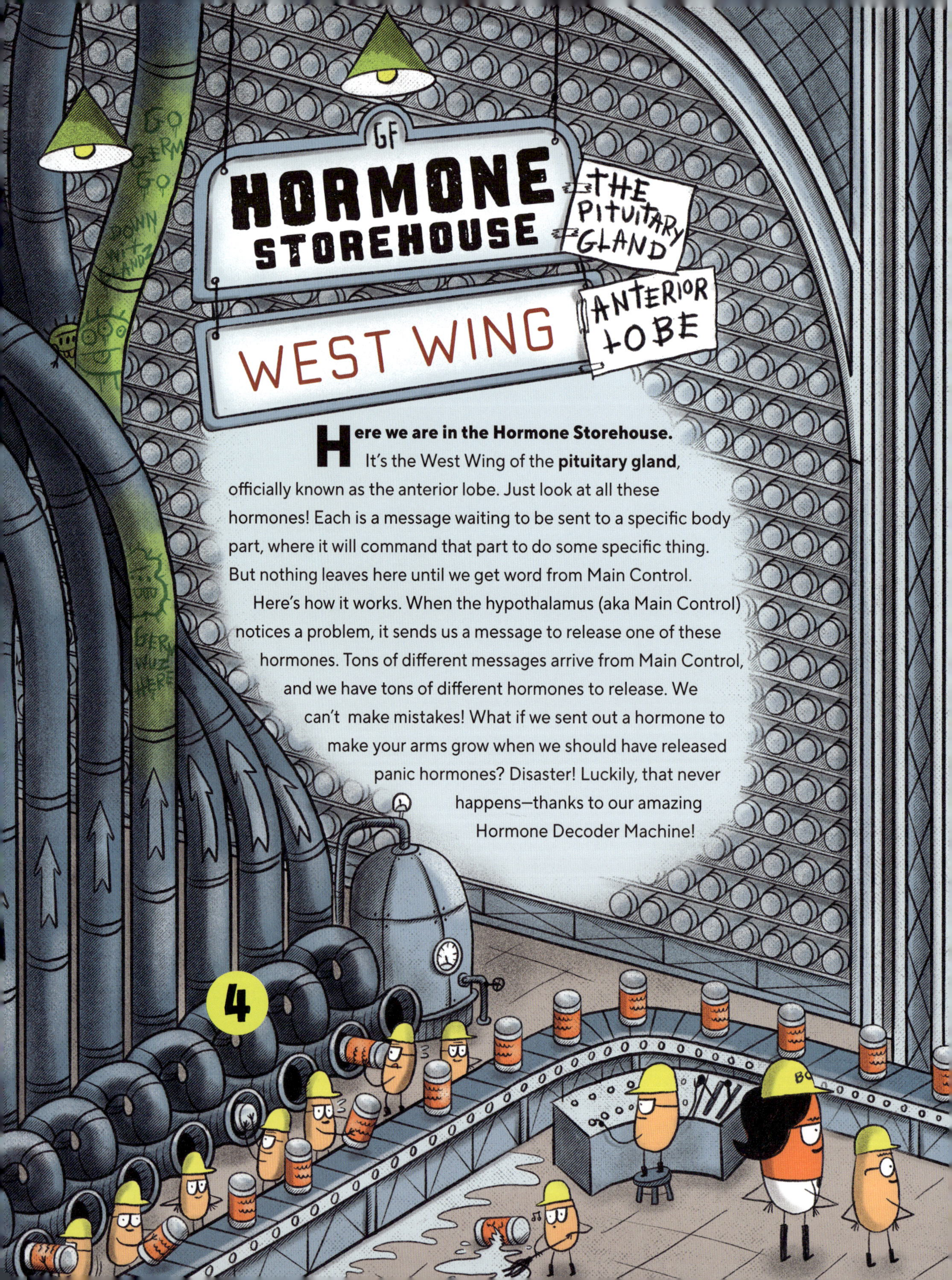

HORMONE STOREHOUSE

WEST WING

Here we are in the Hormone Storehouse. It's the West Wing of the **pituitary gland**, officially known as the anterior lobe. Just look at all these hormones! Each is a message waiting to be sent to a specific body part, where it will command that part to do some specific thing. But nothing leaves here until we get word from Main Control.

Here's how it works. When the hypothalamus (aka Main Control) notices a problem, it sends us a message to release one of these hormones. Tons of different messages arrive from Main Control, and we have tons of different hormones to release. We can't make mistakes! What if we sent out a hormone to make your arms grow when we should have released panic hormones? Disaster! Luckily, that never happens—thanks to our amazing Hormone Decoder Machine!

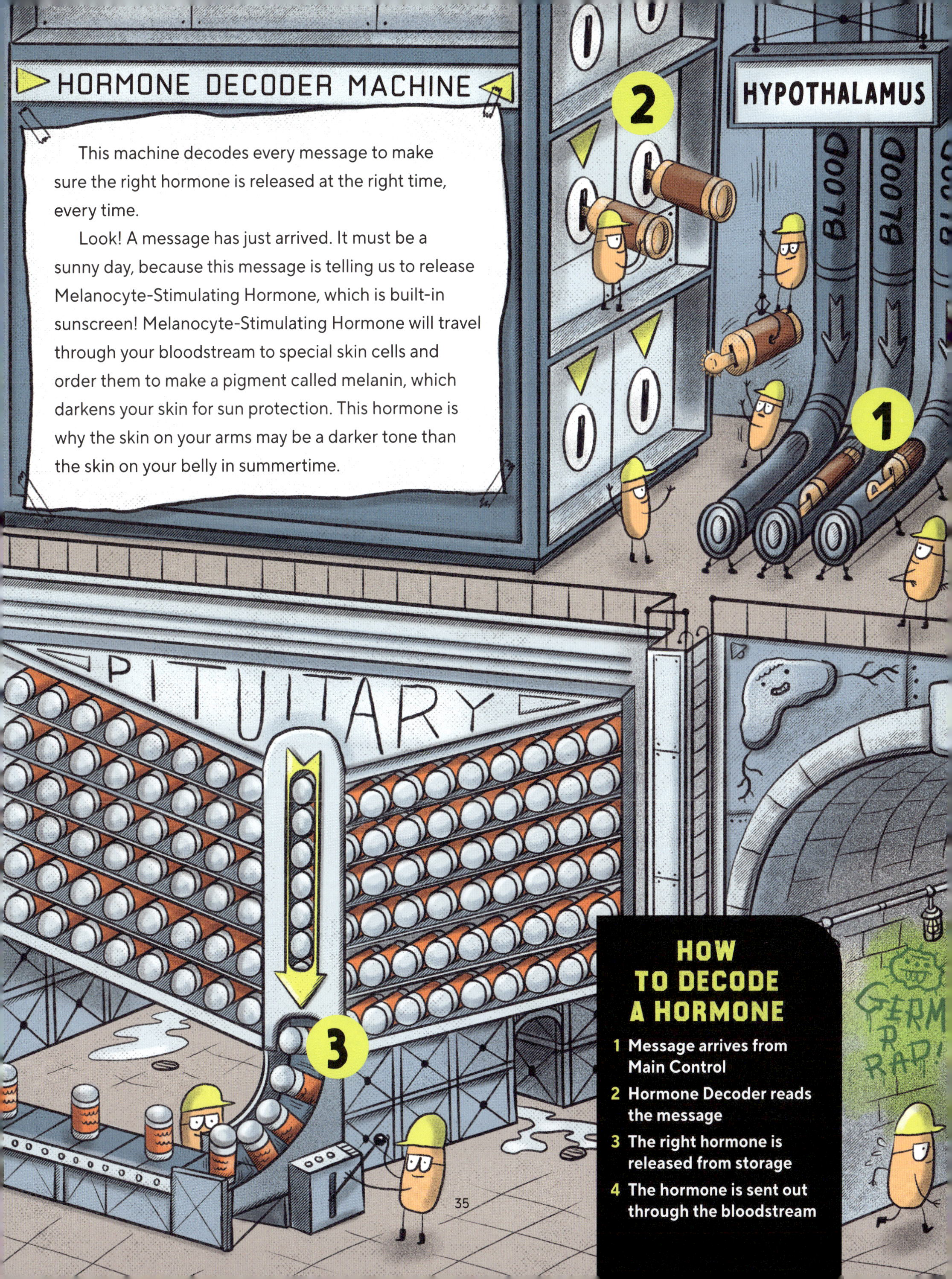

HORMONE DECODER MACHINE

This machine decodes every message to make sure the right hormone is released at the right time, every time.

Look! A message has just arrived. It must be a sunny day, because this message is telling us to release Melanocyte-Stimulating Hormone, which is built-in sunscreen! Melanocyte-Stimulating Hormone will travel through your bloodstream to special skin cells and order them to make a pigment called melanin, which darkens your skin for sun protection. This hormone is why the skin on your arms may be a darker tone than the skin on your belly in summertime.

HOW TO DECODE A HORMONE

1. Message arrives from Main Control
2. Hormone Decoder reads the message
3. The right hormone is released from storage
4. The hormone is sent out through the bloodstream

LH (LUTEINIZING HORMONE)
GERMZ RULE
FISHY
FSH (FOLLICLE-STIMULATING HORMONE)
ARE YOU DOING THIS?
TOO BUSY FOR SCRIBBLES.
TSH (THYROID-STIMULATING HORMONE)
BOSS
TSH
TUSHY
NAME: Thyroid-Stimulating Hormone (TSH) TUSHY
TARGET: Thyroid gland
TUSHY

There are so many important hormones stored here. Like Luteinizing Hormone and Follicle-Stimulating Hormone—their names are so long and windy even scientists just call them LH and FSH. When the order comes from Main Control, we send out LH and FSH, which travel to the **testicles** or **ovaries** (two more Messenger Glands!) and command them to start producing more hormones called testosterone, estrogen, and progesterone. You may have heard of these three before. They're famous because they are sex hormones, and sex hormones—as you know—get *all* the attention.

In any case, when the testicles or ovaries get the message, they begin pumping more testosterone, estrogen, or progesterone into your bloodstream. These hormones circulate around your body and cause all sorts of things to happen. They control processes like puberty, ovulation, and growing babies, but they also give orders for hair to sprout (not just on the top of your head), muscles to grow, and bones to get stronger, and to keep your heart and blood vessels healthy. It's pretty impressive.

This hormone is very important—it's my favorite! Thyroid-Stimulating Hormone, aka TSH. Guess where it's going? Your **thyroid gland**, of course! Your thyroid is a butterfly-shaped Messenger Gland in your throat.

TSH tells your thyroid to release its own hormones—called T3 and T4 (don't worry about their actual names). T3 and T4 then circulate around your body telling each and every cell how hard to work.

The more T3 and T4 you have in your body, the faster your cells change oxygen and nutrients into energy—it's called your metabolic rate. Too much, and your body will go into hyperdrive. Too little, and you'll feel sluggish, tired, and slow. In other words, your thyroid controls how hard and fast your body is working to keep you alive. Like I say, *very* important.

I still haven't answered the all-important question: How does any particular body part know that any particular message is meant for it? What if some skin cells read the wrong message and began sprouting hair instead of turning darker for sun protection?

The answer is so very simple and so very clever. It's a lock and key. Each hormone has a different key that only fits into very specific locks. Thyroid-Stimulating Hormone has a TH key* on the top, while Melanocyte-Stimulating Hormone—that's the one that turns on the tan—has a sunshine-shaped key.

Only your thyroid has the right receptors, or lock, for this TH key. And only skin cells that produce melanin have a sunshine receptor. So, while all hormone messages pass every cell, only the target cells have the right receptors to receive the right message.

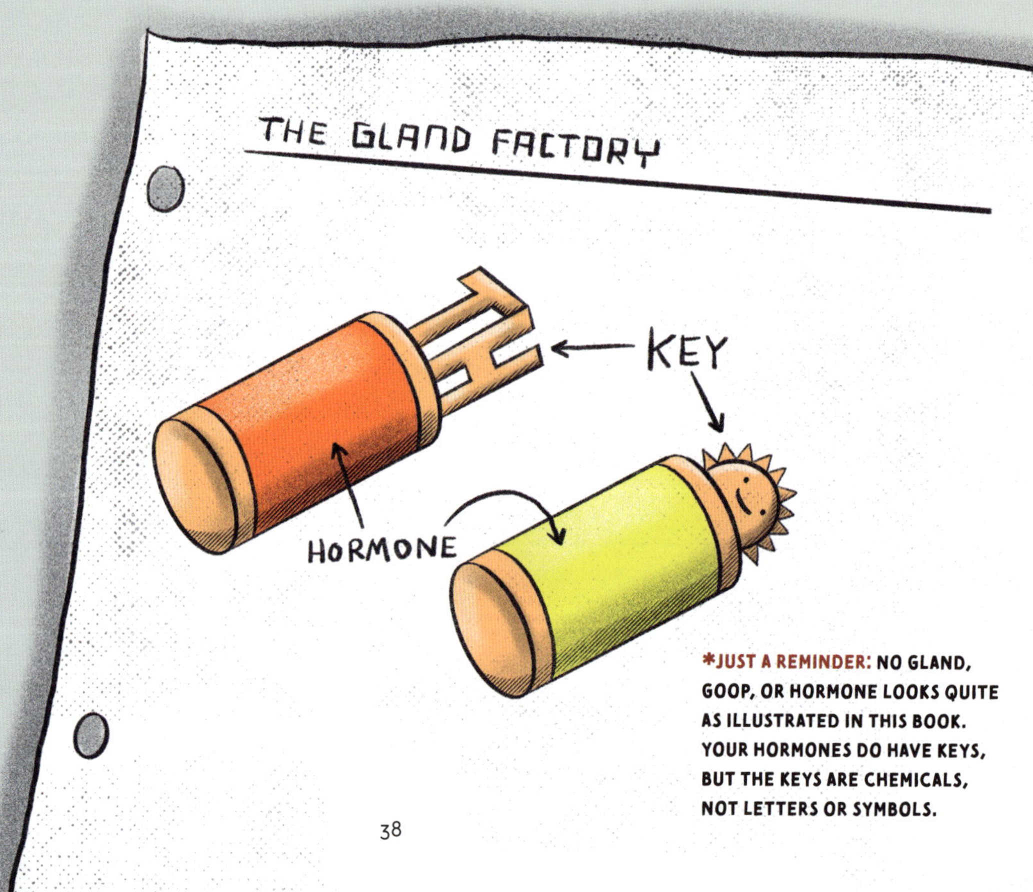

***JUST A REMINDER:** NO GLAND, GOOP, OR HORMONE LOOKS QUITE AS ILLUSTRATED IN THIS BOOK. YOUR HORMONES DO HAVE KEYS, BUT THE KEYS ARE CHEMICALS, NOT LETTERS OR SYMBOLS.

CHECKING IN WITH MAIN CONTROL.
ALL SYSTEMS OKAY?
INTERCOM
healthy
parched
bloated
WATER
healthy
ice cube
roast beef
TEMPERATURE
healthy
mabye dead
about to blow
BLOOD PRESSURE
GERMZ RULE
healthy
activate army
GERM ALERT
INTERCOM
BOSS
BOSS, WE'VE GOT A WATER PROBLEM.
TEMPERATURE IS HIGH AND WATER IS LOW.
INTERCO
BOSS
WATER! NOW!
TO THE EAST WING!

It's a hot day, and you've been sweating to keep cool. Your water is low.

Water, as you probably know, is more important than important. Your body is 60 percent water—and not just the liquidy parts like blood, sweat, and tears. Your heart, brain, and lungs are also mostly water. Even your bones are 30 percent water.

When one body system moves away from Just Right, it can start a cascade of problems across other body systems. Low water means your blood has less water in it, which can cause your blood pressure to go down. And that isn't good. Low blood pressure can mean blood isn't pumping as quickly to bring oxygen and important nutrients to your cells. I've said it before, and I'll say it again—everything in your body is connected. No part of the factory works alone!

You should drink a glass of water. Your hypothalamus has already sent a message to your brain about that, which is why you feel thirsty. And look, your hypothalamus has delivered hormones with a W-shaped key—that's the Anti-Diuretic Hormone. A diuretic is something that makes you pee—which removes water from your body. An *anti*-diuretic is something that stops you from peeing—to keep more water in.

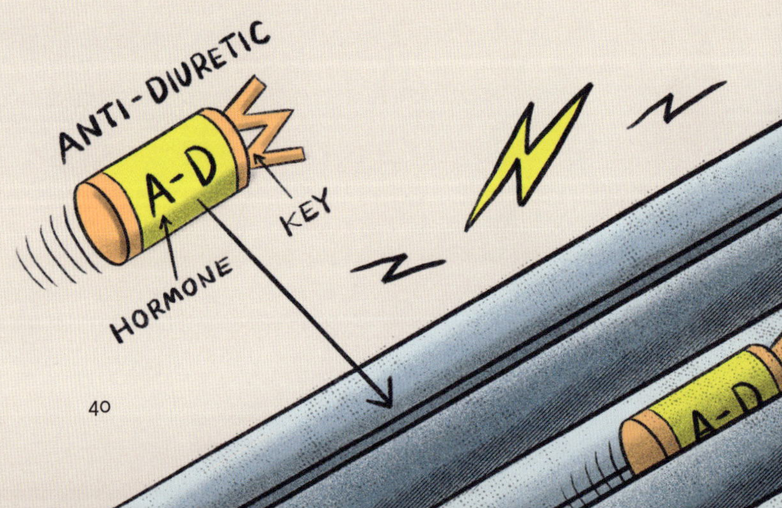

The East Wing of the pituitary—or the posterior lobe—works differently than the West Wing. We don't store any hormones here. Instead, Main Control sends us all the hormones it wants to release. Don't ask me why it doesn't just release them itself. The body is weird sometimes. But all we have to do is take the hormones from the nerve tube and put them into the bloodstream.

Now, let's head down to the kidneys to see the Anti-Diuretic Hormone in action.

NO PEE-PEE HORMONE

ANTI-DIURETIC HORMONE

I'll start with the basics: kidneys are bean-shaped, you have two of them, and they are both amazing.

Each kidney has 1 million tiny filters called nephrons—that's 2 million nephrons in total! Their job is to clean the blood, filter out gunk, and keep just the right balance of water, salts, and other minerals in your blood. It's a big job, and the nephrons never stop working. Every drop of blood in your body is filtered, re-filtered, and filtered again *every five minutes*. Amazing! Let me explain how it works.

Dirty blood is pumped into your kidneys.

Blood flows through a tangled ball of veins and passes through the filters.

Gunk and excess water are drained out while clean and balanced blood circulates back to the body.

Once we receive the No Pee-Pee order—I mean the Anti-Diuretic order—we open these valves, which drain water that was on its way to be peed out back into your blood. Don't worry, it's perfectly clean! This recycling keeps your blood pressure as normal as possible.

In the short term this is perfectly fine, but it will turn your pee darker on hot and thirsty days because your pee has less water to dilute the gunk. Dark pee is your body telling you to drink. Your first morning pee is often dark too. That's because you haven't had water all night, and your body makes extra No Pee-Pee Hormone while you're sleeping so you don't need to pee. Smart, isn't it?

KNOW YOUR SIGNS + SYSTEMS

P TEST

URINE COLOR

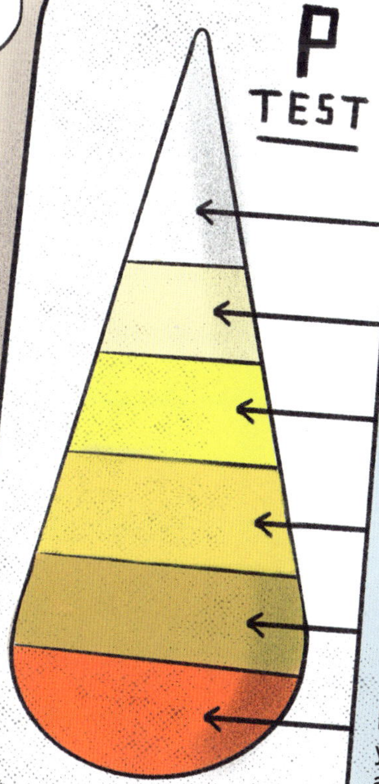

Clear: You're drinking too much water.

Pale yellow: Just Right.

Brilliant yellow: Some vitamins can turn your pee neon yellow.

Medium yellow: Drink a glass of water.

Dark yellow: Drink two glasses of water!

Red: Did you eat beets yesterday? If not, there might be a little blood in your urine. Time to visit the doctor.

ALERT!
EYE 01
TIGER DETECTED
ROAR
4
WHAT'S HAPPENING?
THE EYEBALLS ARE PICKING UP A TIGER.
BREATHING
METABOLISM
SUGAR
GERM ALERT
PANIC
ALERT!!!
BO
ALL STATIONS PREPARE FOR PANIC MODE IN 3 – 2 – 1.
CLICK
PANIC MODE! PANIC MODE!
ALL WORKERS TO THEIR STATIONS!
ROAR
BOSS
THE EARS HAVE DETECTED ROARING.
A TIGER?!
BOSS
PANIC

PANIC MODE!

Don't worry! Insta-Panic is truly instant—we'll escape that tiger! In fact, panic is one of the things your hypothalamus does best. Did I already mention your hypothalamus is in control of your Autonomic Nervous System? I can't remember. It doesn't matter. All you need to know is that it regulates all the processes that seem to *just happen* automatically—like your heartbeat or breathing. It has two basic modes: Panic Mode and Steady Mode. And your hypothalamus can switch between the two at lightning speed.

The hypothalamus has already sent Insta-Zap messages throughout your nervous system to activate Panic Mode. Your heart is beating faster and your lungs have expanded, which means more oxygen is flowing faster through your body. Your **liver** has released more glucose, or sugar, into your blood so your cells will have more readily available fuel. Your pupils are dilated to improve your vision. We've also halted your digestion and sent more blood to your muscles for a faster escape.

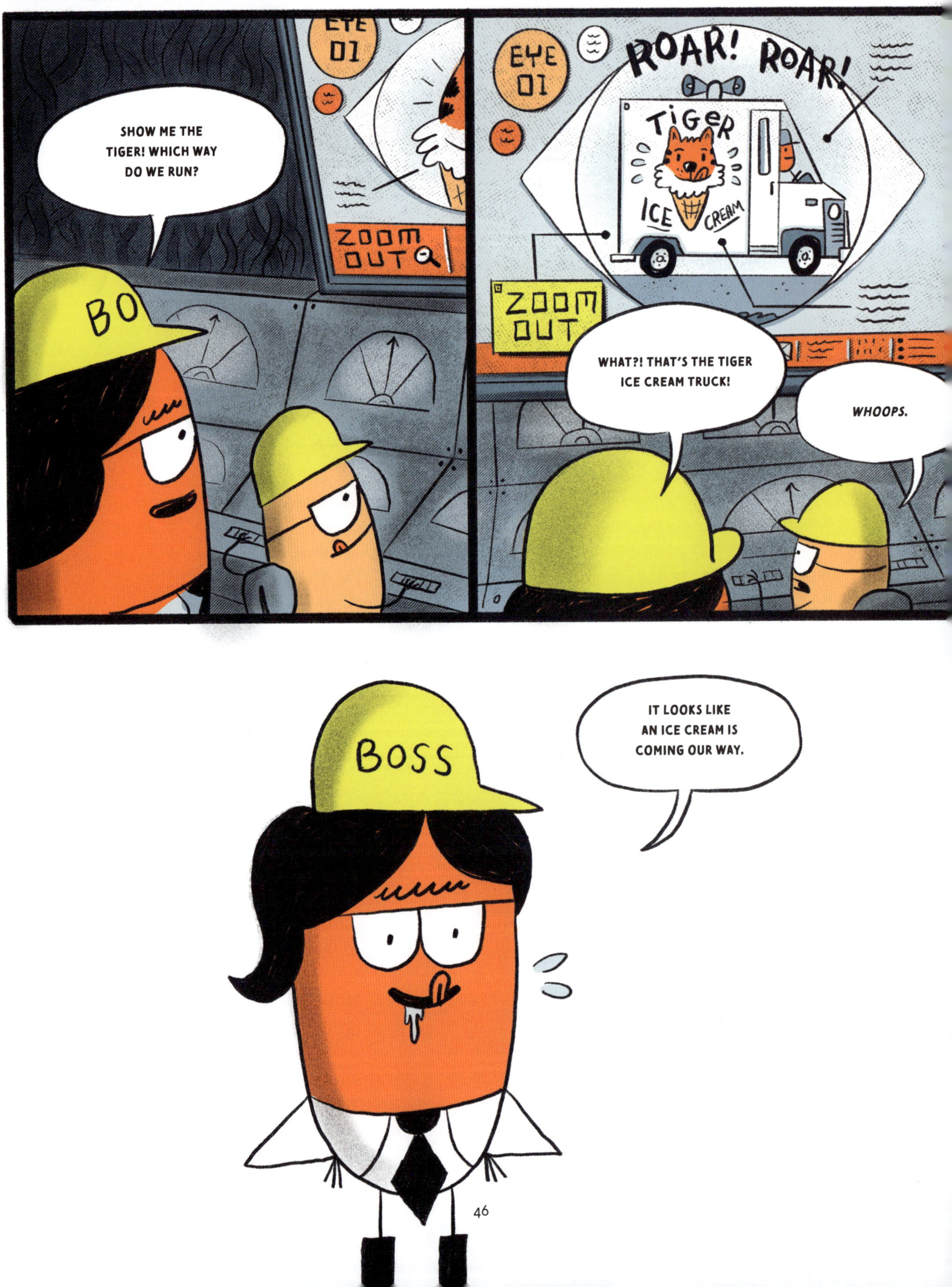

SHOW ME THE TIGER! WHICH WAY DO WE RUN?

ROAR! ROAR!

WHAT?! THAT'S THE TIGER ICE CREAM TRUCK!

WHOOPS.

THE AUTONOMIC NERVOUS SYSTEM

Your Autonomic Nervous System is a network of nerves that regulates unconscious processes, like heartbeat, digestion, and pulse. It has two basic modes. The sympathetic system controls Panic Mode (the "fight or flight" responses) and prepares the body for action. The parasympathetic system regulates Steady Mode (the "rest and digest" functions) and helps the body relax and run life-sustaining processes.

Panic is so important for your survival—or used to be in the age of saber-tooth tigers and cave bears—that your body has several different panic modes. Insta-Panic, Continued Insta-Panic, and Extreme Everlasting Panic.

We've seen how Insta-Panic works. The hypothalamus receives danger signals from your senses—a loud bang, the smell of smoke—and it instantaneously sends PANIC! through your nervous system to body parts that will handle the danger.

If you look at the Panic Mode panel, you'll notice your **adrenal glands** also get the Insta-Panic zap. Your adrenals are Messenger Glands. Once they get the zap, they send out a hormone called adrenaline to all those same organs to make sure they continue panicking. Because adrenal glands send adrenaline through your blood, it lasts longer. Insta-Zaps through your nerves are instant jolts. But adrenaline continues to loop around in the bloodstream until it's all gone. That's Continued Insta-Panic.

But there is another level of panic: Extreme Everlasting Panic. For this one, the hypothalamus sends a hormone to the pituitary, which sends a hormone to the adrenals, which release a different hormone called cortisol. Complicated, I know. Scientists call it the HPA axis (Hypothalamus-Pituitary-Adrenal). I call it the Axis of Doom.

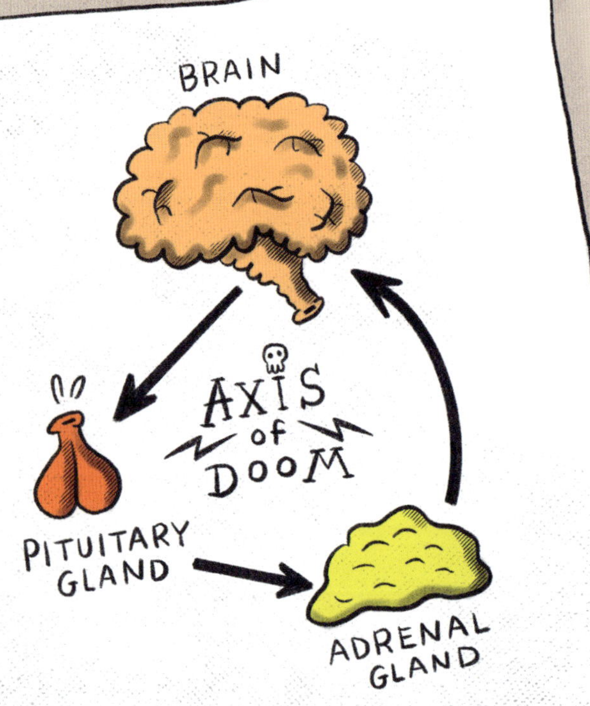

PANIC MODE
PUPILS
WIDE OPEN
STEADY
HEART
FASTER
STEADY
LUNGS
FASTER
STEADY
DIGESTIVE SYSTEM
HALT
STEADY
SALIVARY GLANDS
HALT
STEADY
LIVER
ACTIVATE ENERGY
STEADY
BLADDER
P
SQUEEZE
STEADY
ADRENAL GLANDS
AHHH!
MORE PANIC
STEADY
AUTONOMIC NERVOUS SYSTEM
AXIS OF X DOOM
BLOOD 01
BLOOD 02
BLOOD 03
BLOOD 04
WHOOPS.
WHOOPS.
HORMONE RELEASE
HORMONE RELEASE
HORMONE RELEASE
BLOOD
BLOOD

To be clear, cortisol is always floating around your body. You have higher levels in the morning to help you wake up and lower levels in the evening to help you slow down. Almost every cell in your body has a receptor for it, and it affects almost every body system. But when extreme panic causes your body to pump out extra cortisol, it can shut down systems that aren't strictly necessary for your immediate survival.

Like, for example, your Infection Detection Immune System, which fights disease and infection. It's really important for long-term survival, but it uses a lot of energy, and who cares about a runny nose when you're running for your life? And sex hormones—you don't need those to escape a tiger. Cortisol also tells the liver to release more sugars into your blood, increases your blood pressure, and affects how your muscles and tissues deal with injury, all in order to help you survive immediate dangers.

As you can imagine, too many panic hormones circulating for too long is bad for your health. But don't worry, the panic is over. Your cortisol levels will soon dwindle back down until the next emergency, which always seems to be right around the corner.

Wait! What? Blood sugars are too high? Never a moment's rest!

PANIC AND FEAR

Pale face: Face turns pale as less blood flows to outer ranges (because more blood is needed for vital organs and muscles in emergencies).

Butterflies: Stomach feels fluttery as less blood flows to the digestive system.

Shaky muscles: Muscles quiver as adrenaline prepares them to contract quickly, if running is required.

Pee-pee: Muscles of the bladder tense, which makes you want to pee.

Dry mouth: Less saliva as digestive system halts and more water shifts to other systems, like sweat glands.

DIGESTION DEPARTMENT
THE PANCREAS
STOMACH
LIVER
GALL-BLADDER
PANCREAS
TO MOUTH MACHINE
BOSS
POOPVILLE

Blood sugar is exactly what it sounds like: sugar in your blood. Sugar, or glucose, is your body's main source of energy. But like everything else, your blood sugar needs to be kept at Just Right levels—not too much, not too little. You've eaten an ice cream and a doughnut, and we dumped a load of stored sugar into your blood during Panic Mode. No wonder your levels are high. But we've got just the gland to get it under control: Sugar Boss!

Sugar Boss is part of the Digestion Department. We don't have time to talk about digestion, but you should know there's a hardworking gland every step of the way—from the very top to the very bottom (if you know what I mean).

GERMZ #1
ALERT!
THIZ IZ GERM TOWN
DIGESTION DEPARTMENT
LIVER
GALL-BLADDER
PANCREAS
BOSS
HAVE YOU SEEN THEM BEFORE?
YES! T-CELLS ARE ON THEIR WAY.

GERMZ RULE
KING GERM
I ♥ POOPVILLE
POOP

Your Infection Detection Immune System is an incredible security network of glands, organs, tissues, and cells, so intricate and complicated that even I don't fully understand how it all works. The first line of defense is your Defender Goops: your mucus, saliva, and stomach acid. You already met a few of these guys. They are very good at killing germs on contact. If any germs do sneak past them, your police cells take over.

You see, your Infection Detection team has a massive force of different police cells constantly monitoring your body and watching for bad agents. In charge are police chiefs called T-cells. T-cells are trained to know and destroy every bad germ and to make sure the right police cells are dealing with any particular attack.

You'll be please to know that T-cells are trained by the **thymus gland**—yet another Messenger Gland. The thymus is like a police academy teaching young T-cells to recognize good cells from bad germs and how to fight each specific germ.

We've seen these germs before, or at least ones very much like them. They gave you that runny nose last year. Because the T-cells have been trained to deal with them, they'll make sure the germs are rounded up and destroyed before they cause any nasty symptoms.

ATTACK CONTAINED!
PHEW! UNDER CONTROL.

WE BEAT 'EM BEFORE
WE'LL BEAT 'EM AGAIN
BUT WE NEED YOU

BOSS, BLOOD SUGAR LEVELS ARE STILL HIGH.
ACK! I FORGOT. NO TIME TO DELAY.
BOSS

SUGAR BOSS
PANCREAS, AGAIN!
SB
GOOP
IN
OUT
SUGAR
CANDY
BOSS

Ah, the pancreas! What a star! It's both a Goop Gland and a Messenger Gland. As a Goop Gland, it helps digest your food. As a Messenger Gland, it's known around here as Sugar Boss. It deals with what happens once that food—specifically the sugar—hits your bloodstream.

Sugar Boss monitors the amount of sugar in your blood and releases different hormones to make sure your levels stay at Just Right. When your blood sugar is high, Sugar Boss releases a hormone called insulin. Insulin tells your cells to take in sugar from the bloodstream. Your cells may use the sugar right away as fuel or store it until it's needed. Either way, insulin is required to move sugar from your bloodstream into your cells. Once your cells have used or stored the sugar, and your blood sugar falls back to Just Right, Sugar Boss stops releasing insulin. Scientists call this a negative feedback loop. I just call it good management. It's how much of the factory is run, and how we keep homeostasis and all systems running smooth and stable.

Sugar Boss works the other way too. If sugar levels are low, it releases a hormone called glucagon, which tells your cells, muscles, and liver to release their stored sugar into your blood for ready use.

Since your sugar levels are high after eating doughnuts and ice cream, we'll release more insulin, and quick as a pop you'll be back to Just Right.

Finally, all systems are stable! For the moment. We've got one last stop on the tour. Thankfully, it's a calm one. Let's take the elevator this time.

Our last stop on the tour. Sleepy-Time Central, also known as your **pineal gland**. It all starts with your 24-hour clock in Main Control. This clock has a fabulous name. Suprachiasmatic Nucleus! That's *Supra-keye-as-matic New-klee-us*, in case you were wondering. So fancy. I love saying it.

Suprachiasmatic Nucleus gets constant updates from your eyeballs about what the sun is doing. Is the sun rising? Is it the middle of the night? These updates are sent to Main Control, which uses them to synchronize all your body systems to a daily rhythm of wakefulness and sleepiness, known as your circadian rhythm, which is also fun to say. Try it: *Sir-ka-dee-an ryth-imm.*

As nighttime approaches, Main Control gets the body ready for sleep. It slows your heart rate, lowers your levels of cortisol to help you fall asleep, and sends a message here, to Sleepy-Time Central.

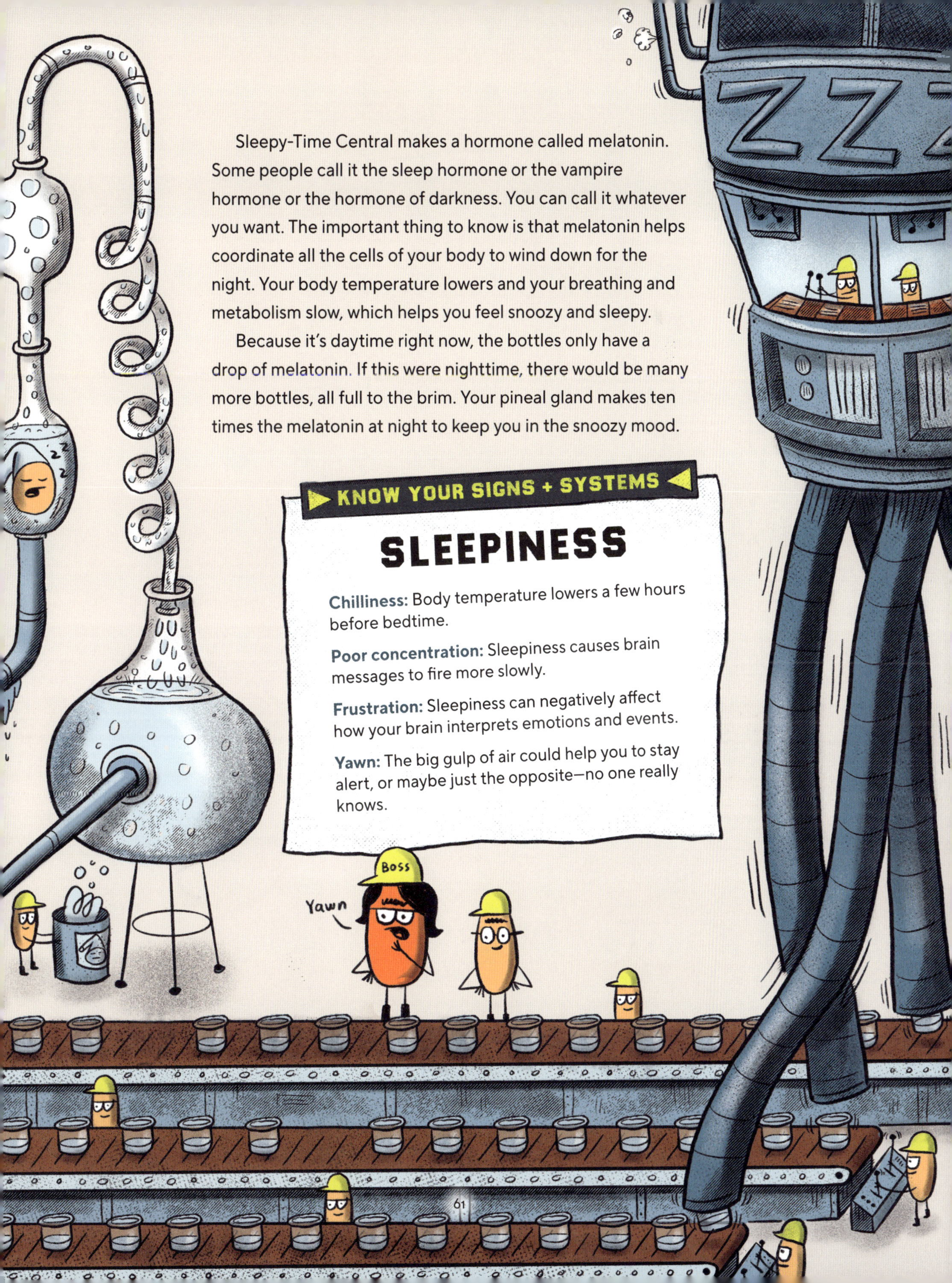

Sleepy-Time Central makes a hormone called melatonin. Some people call it the sleep hormone or the vampire hormone or the hormone of darkness. You can call it whatever you want. The important thing to know is that melatonin helps coordinate all the cells of your body to wind down for the night. Your body temperature lowers and your breathing and metabolism slow, which helps you feel snoozy and sleepy.

Because it's daytime right now, the bottles only have a drop of melatonin. If this were nighttime, there would be many more bottles, all full to the brim. Your pineal gland makes ten times the melatonin at night to keep you in the snoozy mood.

KNOW YOUR SIGNS + SYSTEMS

SLEEPINESS

Chilliness: Body temperature lowers a few hours before bedtime.

Poor concentration: Sleepiness causes brain messages to fire more slowly.

Frustration: Sleepiness can negatively affect how your brain interprets emotions and events.

Yawn: The big gulp of air could help you to stay alert, or maybe just the opposite—no one really knows.

THROUGH THE WAXY EAR HOLES

Look at the time! I really must get back to the business of being busy! The Gland Factory doesn't just run itself.

There is much more to see and so much more to explain, but I'm afraid this concludes our tour. I hope you enjoyed seeing our many divisions and departments and the endless roller coaster of your internal workings. Aren't you glad to know your glands are forever working hard to keep you gliding smoothly through life? We are such an exciting bunch.

You may exit to the left or right, through the Waxy Ear Holes.

Before you go, please consider having a look at our visitor survey. We would love to know how you enjoyed the tour and what we could improve. Here at the factory, we are always striving to do better. Forever watching! Forever fixing! Because we are the Gland Factory!

LEFT
PULL FOR WAX
EXIT
SURVEY

GLAND FACTORY SURVEY

1. How did you feel on the tour? Choose all that apply.

Fascinated
Confused
Flabbergasted
Disgusted
Bored

2. What was your favorite goop?

Snot
Sebum
Saliva
Whose Bum
Meibum
Other

3. What were your favorite gland activities?

Swelling
Dripping
Cooling
Defending
Spraying
Shrinking
Moisturizing
Warming
Balancing
Squeezing
Oozing
Panicking!
Healing
Spewing
Snoozing

4. Would you be interested in working at the factory? If so, in what department?

LIBRARIANS EVERYWHERE SAY "PLEASE DO NOT WRITE IN THIS BOOK!"

GLOSSARY

A **gland** is an organ that makes one or more substances, such as hormones, digestive juices, sweat, tears, saliva, or milk. There are two gland systems.

1. **Messenger Glands** (endocrine glands) release hormone messages into the bloodstream. Many parts of the body that are not glands also produce hormones, such as the kidneys, fatty tissues, and the intestines.

2. **Goop Glands** (exocrine glands) release goop or juices directly where they are needed.

And here are your amazing glands, helpfully listed in alphabetical order. You've already seen a few of them in action, while others are yet to be explored.

Adrenal glands are Messenger Glands that help regulate your metabolism, immune system, blood pressure, and stress response.

Ceruminous glands are Goop Glands that make earwax.

The **hypothalamus** (Main Control) is a Messenger Gland that monitors, regulates, and coordinates bodily systems to keep you working smoothly and steadily.

Lacrimal glands are a group of Goop Glands that make different liquids to moisturize and protect your eyeballs.

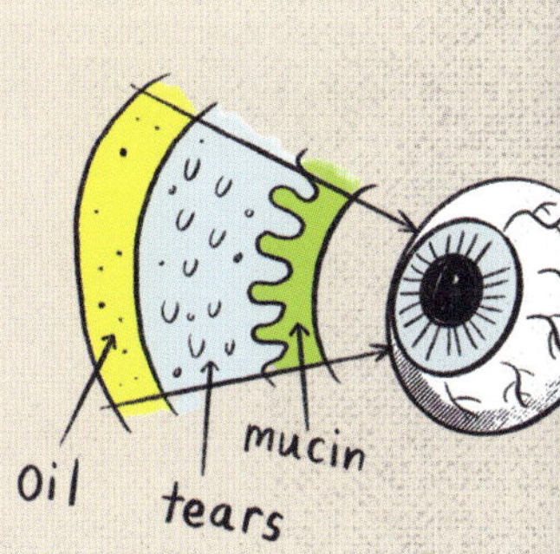

The **liver** has two roles: As a Goop Gland it makes bile to help digestion. As a Messenger Gland it makes many vital hormones.

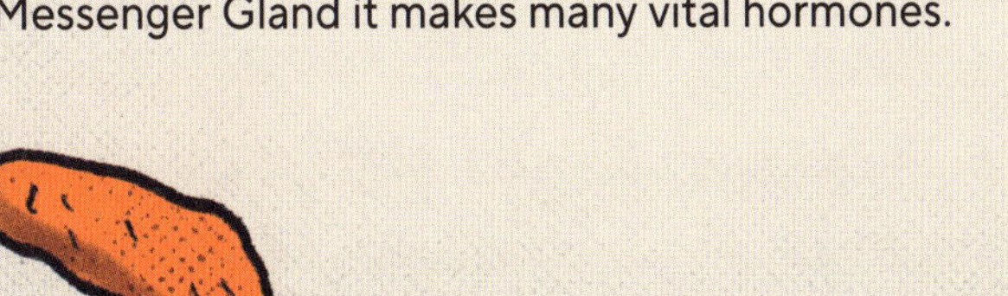

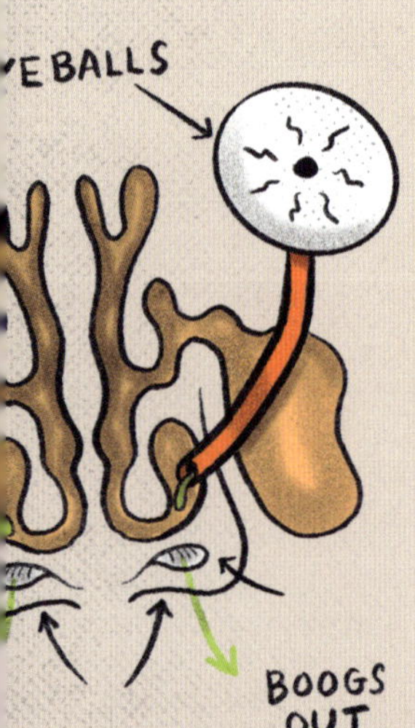

Mammary glands are Goop Glands that make milk. The hormones that start the process usually begin with pregnancy.

Mucous glands are Goop Glands that cover all body parts where Insides meet the Outside, including the entire length of your respiratory and digestive tracts.

Mucus is a sticky, goopy substance made by mucous glands to moisten and protect.

Nasal glands are Goop Glands that make mucus to moisturize and clean the air you breathe, protect your nose, and enable the sense of smell.

Ovaries have two roles: As Goop Glands they release eggs. As Messenger Glands they make hormones important for female sexual development, fertility, and pregnancy.

The **pancreas** has two main functions: As a Goop Gland it makes digestive juices. As a Messenger Gland, it's Sugar Boss and controls the amount of sugar in your bloodstream.

The **parathyroid gland** is a Messenger Gland that regulates your blood level of calcium and phosphorus.

The **pineal gland** (Sleepy-Time Central) is a Messenger Gland that makes the hormone melatonin to help regulate your sleep cycle.

The **pituitary gland** (the Storehouse) is a Messenger Gland that releases many important hormones and controls the function of many other glands. It has two lobes known as the West Wing (anterior lobe) and East Wing (posterior lobe).

PITUITARY GLAND

Salivary glands are Goop Glands that make saliva to moisturize and protect your mouth, kill germs, and help dissolve and swallow food.

Sweat glands are Goop Glands that help regulate body temperature with sweat.

The **testicles** (testes) have two roles: As Goop Glands they make sperm. As Messenger Glands they make hormones important for the male reproductive system as well as the growth of bone, muscle, and hair.

The **thymus gland** is a Messenger Gland that filters and monitors blood contents. It also trains special white blood cells called T-cells to fight disease and infection.

The **thyroid gland** is a Messenger Gland that regulates the body's metabolic rate, growth, and development. It also helps control the heart, muscle and digestive function, brain development, and bone maintenance.

FURTHER READING

It Takes Guts: How Your Body Turns Food Into Fuel (And Poop) by Dr. Jennifer Gardy, illustrated by Belle Wuthrich (Greystone Kids, 2021)

Thirty Trillion Cells: How Your Body Really Works by Isabel Thomas, illustrated by Dawn Cooper (Welbeck Editions, 2022)

The Ultimate Human Body Encyclopedia: The Complete Visual Guide to How Your Body Works by Jon Richards (Welbeck Children's, 2022)

INDEX

This index is like a map, showing you where to find information inside this book. You can use it by looking for a subject that interests you, like "taste buds" or "meibum" or "Goop Glands." All of the main headings are in alphabetical order. The numbers after each key word are the page numbers where you will find information. Page numbers in a range (for example, 54–55) tell you that information is found on pages 54 *and* 55.

BIOS

Rachel Poliquin writes award-winning nonfiction children's books about science, nature, and animals—but with a twist. Pythons are on roller skates. Wisdom teeth talk. And there is a witch at the bottom of the sea. Her recent books include *I Am Wind: An Autobiography* and *The Museum of Odd Body Leftovers*. She lives in Vancouver with her husband, three children, and an almost-feral cat.

Clayton Hanmer (aka CTON) has illustrated a bunch of other interesting children's books, including *The Museum of Odd Body Leftovers* and *Trending: How and Why Stuff Gets Popular*. He loves old factories, drawing too much detail, and tinkering with machines. At one point, Clayton even lived in an old factory but now lives with his family in a normal house in Bloomfield, Ontario, where they all have a nice collective of glands and germs.

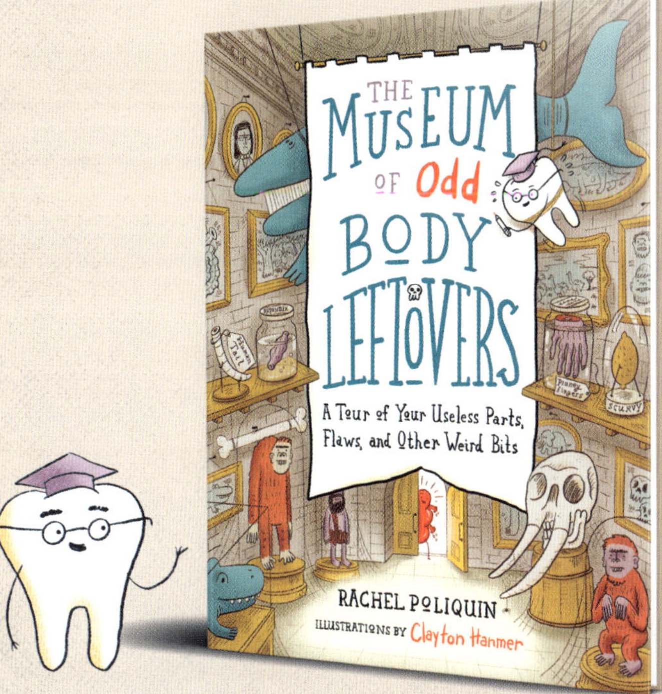

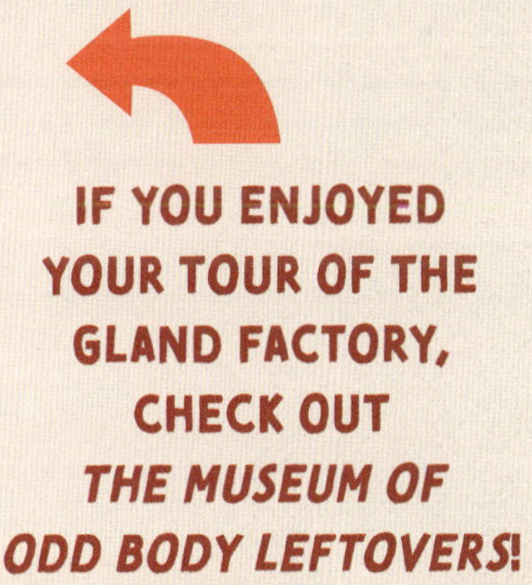

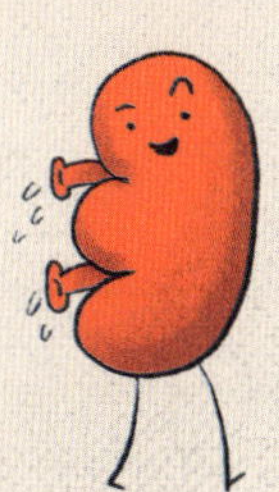

For Beatrice, who gave me the idea
RP

A great big hug and thanks to Sal,
Alice, and Otter for your patience while
I worked all that overtime and
double shifts at the Gland Factory
CTON

25 26 27 28 29   5 4 3 2 1

Greystone Kids / Greystone Books Ltd.
greystonebooks.com

Cataloguing data available from Library and Archives Canada
ISBN 978-1-77840-098-8 (cloth)
ISBN 978-1-77840-099-5 (epub)

Canada

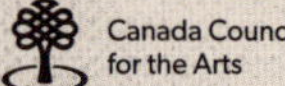

Canada Council for the Arts
Conseil des arts du Canada

Greystone Books gratefully acknowledges the xʷməθkʷəy̓əm (Musqueam), Sḵwx̱wú7mesh (Squamish), and səlilwətaɬ (Tsleil-Waututh) peoples on whose land our Vancouver head office is located.

Editing by Linda Pruessen
Copy editing by Tracy Bordian
Proofreading by Alison Strobel
Indexing by Stephen Ullstrom
Design by Jessica Sullivan | DSGN Dept.
The illustrations in this book were rendered in digital pencil and paint using Procreate.

Special thanks to Dr. Mike Todorovic and Dr. Preetha Krishnamoorthy for their expert review.

Printed and bound in China on FSC® certified paper at Shenzhen Reliance Printing. The FSC® label means that materials used for the product have been responsibly sourced.

Greystone Books thanks the Canada Council for the Arts, the British Columbia Arts Council, the Province of British Columbia through the Book Publishing Tax Credit, and the Government of Canada for supporting our publishing activities.

EU Safety Information: Easy Access System Europe, Mustamäe tee 50, 10621 Tallinn, Estonia, gpsr.requests@easproject.com.

BOSS